"THE PASSIVE INCOME LIE"

Max Musumali

CHAPTER 1: INTRODUCTION

For more than a decade a craze has swept across the world. A promise of something that has been hidden from most of us. Something that we simply didn't know and never really thought about.

Passive income.

Doing work once, in the here and now, and reaping the benefits later. Time and time again.

I came across this concept around 2004. Wandering into my older brother's room I found a book. It wasn't his, it was our fathers. 'Rich Dad, Poor Dad' it was called.

I was too young to make accurate observations about how the world works but I knew one thing. Life doesn't work how we're taught it does. Even as a teenager, I could see how many errors I made in my day to day thinking. Could it be that other people made these errors too?

Around 2008 this passive income thing really gained traction. I got a little obsessed studying it. I mean, it practically sounds like magic. And in many ways it was...

I vaguely remember being told about some book called 'The 4 Hour Work Week'. I didn't finish reading it. Taking one look at how thick it was, I thought it better to read my school book. I failed my exams, but at least I made it look like I tried.

A system of making money that actually pays you what you're worth. Magic. I couldn't get that out of my head. That was always the problem you see. Nothing ever seemed fair. Whatever you're paid for a job is always ten times less than what you're worth to your boss or company.

That's what got me fired up about passive income. Over time you can build a portfolio. Even if it wasn't much money, you'd get it over an extended period of time. It pays you what you're worth, it just takes time.

Let's admit that the idea of waking up every morning and having made a couple of bucks is quite exciting.

Much of the world was as excited as I was.

Bit by bit success stories came out. People who were living the passive income dream. They started on their hustle on the side and made it happen. They screwed the system that is designed to screw you.

It was awesome. Pure magic.

Then I stopped, stepped back and took a breather for a second. They say never follow the herd. Could it be that somewhere along its road to popularity this concept lost touch with reality? It had happened before. In fact, it seems to happen a lot.

No.

It didn't lose itself along the way. The idea of passive income that was being pushed onto us was never right to begin with. It was a craze. An illusion, just like stage magic!

A craze that took advantage of the times. A craze that took advantage of hopes and dreams. Frustrations and pain. A craze that helped usher in a new wave of financial independence, but it was still only a craze. An illusion!

Crazes don't last. You want to build something that lasts. Something that moves you forward in life. Something that makes you happy.

"Doesn't passive income do this?" you might ask. Yes it does. Only the way we think of passive income today is not adequate. It's false and holds you back. That's not only dangerous, it's sad. It's sad because the misconceptions will kill your growth as an entrepreneur and human being. By thinking of passive income the way the mainstream does, we're holding ourselves back.

Let's see if we can change that.

That's what "The Passive Income Lie" is all about. It's time to get things straight!

CHAPTER 2: IS THE WAY WE THINK RIGHT?

It's been years since I read, "Rich Dad, Poor Dad". In case you're not familiar with it it's the story of how the author learned about life and wealth from his two 'dads'. One was his biological father, Poor Dad. A man who was a well-educated employee for all of his life. The other was his best friend's father, Rich Dad. Less educated but savvy where business is concerned.

Robert Kiyosaki (the author) talks about all the great things his Rich Dad taught him. Things that most people never seem to notice and how they are always different from the norm. The norm being what his Poor Dad tried to teach him.

Kiyosaki's things was real-estate. In the book he suggested ways to escape from the day to day hardships of life, to starting your own business. He also talked about passive income. This was one of the first sources a many people ever came across regarding the matter. There was somewhat of a 'Rich Dad mania' at the time –video courses, board games and seminars soon followed.

The decentralization of information can be a beautiful thing. The so called 'rich' didn't have the monopoly on these juicy secrets anymore.

However, there was a slight issue.

The type of issue that leads to bad debt and being thrown out of your home. The overall advice that Kiyosaki gave was sound. Start a business if you want to get rich. Simple. Invest in real-estate. Simple. The problem was that a lot of the detailed action steps in his program where...rubbish! Just plain bad if you think about it.

That didn't matter so much though because he had spurred on a lot of people to take their financial life into their own hands. People were now aware that passive income existed and many scampered around looking for such opportunities. By the way, Kiyosaki's business declared bankruptcy a while ago.

Another significant person that shaped how we think of passive income today is a guy called Timothy Ferriss. The fellow who wrote "The 4 Hour Work Week".

I know it's ridiculous to attribute the discovery of passive income to these two guys but they did have a profound effect on popular culture and awareness. They are more like representations of the thoughts that were floating around at the time.

Ferriss was different because he was an innovator. A sharp lad who thought of things in his own unique way and loved the good life. In his book he talked about how one can set up a business and, eventually, get away with working only 4 hours a week. It reflects on how you can use the internet and leverage outsourcing to build yourself a passive income stream.

He went into great detail. It's obvious how much work he put into the book. That work was reflected by its success. It was a massive success. It was so successful that people he mentioned in the book can attribute a good deal of their ensuing success to being mentioned in it.

You are a sharp reader. So you probably asked yourself, "How can he say this when he didn't bother finishing the book?" The answer is simple. I didn't need to. There are some things you can't run away from. Like a flood, an earthquake or flu. In the self-development world Ferriss was the most effective strain of flu ever.

Unlike Kiyosaki, Ferris was charismatic and knew how to engage people. The concept spread like wild fire and more and more younger people decided to start their own businesses. His ideas were also much more refined and practical. These are things that he had tried himself. They worked.

Yet, once again, there was a slight issue.

Not the kind were you get thrown out of your house though (thank God). Suddenly you had all these people saying they want to build passive income based business. Most of these where young. They wanted to build passive income because in their heads passive income meant you get to work less. It even meant you don't need to work at all. They called this "lifestyle-design".

Now you have a generation that is convinced that passive income is the key to the good life. You can go as far as saying that they think that passive income is an entitlement. "How dare you make me work for 8 hours a day, 5 days a week?!"

That's scary.

People in their 20s and 30s are essentially lazy. They want to do a bit of work and profit from it for the rest of their lives. Worst is I'm one of them and it took a lot to beat that mentality out of me. I'm not blaming Tim Ferriss for the retardation of an entire generation. I'm just saying that's some crazy stuff.

We're so lazy.

On the other hand the same lazy youngsters are building new businesses left, right and center. The world as a whole has never been as innovative as it is now. Entrepreneurship is becoming a social norm. Go back 50 years and you could have been disowned and banished for wanting to start your own business.

So we have people starting clever new ventures that have no work ethic whatsoever.

Hmm.

This problem might be a bit bigger than we first thought.

People can't be that lazy and entitled and brilliant at the same time can they? Unfortunately they can. Especially if society already rewards such behavior.

Ask yourself this question. How many people that you know genuinely like their jobs? Not love. Not content. Just like.

The truth is that having a job is not what it used to be. There's no such thing as job security. There's no such thing as moving up the ladder. We work because we have to, not because we want to. Jobs aren't fun.

That's like a general thing everyone agrees with to some extent. This is what so many people experience. This is also what society teaches us. We are literally taught that jobs aren't fun. Work is not fun. It's serious, because where work is concerned fun and seriousness are mutually exclusive.

What a bunch of bull crap.

The entrepreneurial generation of today isn't building businesses because they want to or are crazy passionate. We're building them because we don't want to be sad all the time. Being sad sucks. Why would you do something every day that makes you feel like you're worthless?

Heck, the job could be alright but when you feel oppressed what can you do? A big part of entrepreneurship in the 21st century is not about building something, it's about running away from something.

The flip side is that there is a lot of entitlement going around these days. What else can happen if we're told time and time again how special we are?

That's why the idea of passive income has exploded the way it has. Feelings of anger and entitlement.

Passive income is about refusing to play the game the way it has been played all along. Or rather it is choosing to play an entirely different type of game.

Even though my ranting has sounded pessimistic so far, overall everything is positive. We tend to let negative emotions lead us. If these end up leading us to more prosperity it's a good thing. BUT we want to get better and not be stuck with limiting beliefs.

If you are confused how we got from books to a psychologically damaged generation you are not alone. I too am wondering how we got here... at least it seems to make sense.

So let's clear the air. One of our major problems is that we look at work the wrong way. What you do every day shouldn't only drain you. It should energies you as well.

You must have worked on a project before where you dreaded going to bed. Not because you fear an incomplete project but because you just like working on in. Remember having trouble sleeping because your mind is ablaze.

Going to work only for the sake of a paycheck is self-destructive.

Working on something you like, in a good environment is self-development.

That's the real value of the passive income movement. Going after something like this forces you to get out of your comfort zone. In this way today's generation is superior to its forbearers. The young are lazy but more willing to push the boundaries.

All well and good but what does this mean if you want to start making passive income?

Passive income depends heavily on what you want out of life. It's one of those, "It's not about the end, it's about the journey," situations. Yes it's cliché but as this booklet will reveal it will take a while to master this form of income. You need to resolve to not let all the rubbish inside your own head hold you back.

We've been thinking the wrong way. We've chosen to believe the wrong things.

Passive income is not what you think it is and it's time to set the record straight.

If you take anything away from this book let me tell you what it should be. Passive income is the most inferior type of income.

Warning there'll be more trash talking as we dive deeper. God's speed.

Let's first make sure we really understand what passive income is.

CHAPTER 3: DEFINING PASSIVE INCOME

We need to start with defining passive income. Everybody seems to have a different way of looking at it. This isn't necessarily bad, but it does make it harder to make sense of the issue.

First and foremost you need to understand that passive income involves some sort of action in the beginning. Something you do at the start of your project that generates money for you down the line. This money comes in periodically, meaning every once in a while. Maybe every month or every year.

Ideally there should also be a deadline for how long the project supplies you with income. If it's something that only brings in money for three months does it qualify? The answer is, No! Passive income should be medium term, if not a long term source of cash. Medium term is a time span of six months to one year. Long term is a time span of over one year.

Time brings to mind another factor we need to consider. How many times do you have to control your project within its life time? There will always be some sort of maintenance work that needs to be done. You will need to give yourself time to make sure everything is running smoothly. This is something that is often misunderstood about passive income. You don't do the work once and then get rewarded forever and ever. You still need to put in some extra work down the line. If you consider this, then there is no such thing as 'passive' income.

That's why the maintenance work should be relatively easy. Easy for you or easy for someone you're outsourcing too. It may require being a specialist. A project that forces you to work twenty hours a week on it is not passive. Twenty hours isn't much time at all but it's too much time where passive income is concerned.

On the other hand a project that demands only 60 a year is passive income. The difference is that these hours might be spaced out or batched together. It might be something that requires you to pull all-nighters for four days. The most important thing is getting the job done and forgetting about it for a healthy amount of time.

So that means that passive income has three components to consider:

-The starting work

-A lifespan of over 6 months (preferably over 1 year)

- How much maintenance needs to be done.

Maintenance is an issue that will bring up a lot of arguments on this issue. *In fact, maintenance is the most important aspect of passive income*. It is not what you're doing or how much money you make. It's how long and hard the maintenance is.

Here are different definition by some authorities on how they look at it.

"With passive income, you would keep getting paid whether or not you do any meaningful work. You may do a lot of work up front to get the ball rolling, but eventually you reach a point where the passive income stream gets activated. At this point you can essentially stop working on this income stream if you so desire, and more money will keep flowing to you through this stream regardless what you do or don't do."

-Steve Pavlina

*"Building online businesses that take advantage of **systems of automation** that allow **transactions, cash flow,** and **growth** to happen without requiring a real-time presence."*

-Pat Flyn

The one thing that we can be sure of is that passive income is not doing something actively. If you freelance that is not passive income. You get paid for the work you do. If you don't do the work you don't get paid. If you're sick and bed ridden for a month you don't get paid. That's more of a side hustle or side business.

It seems like a lot of people confuse side hustles for passive income. Maybe it's because of the sex appeal. When someone's looking for a way to supplement their income they somehow stumble upon passive income. Then the idea hits, and they try to become briefcases entrepreneur and build a passive income source. Somewhere along the line they mess things up and think they have created passive income when that isn't the case.

I blame the internet. Lots of people spread wisdom that has not been earned in the slightest way and make up random theories. More importantly, there are so (soooooo) many ways to profit of the net via online business. Since this is pretty much a new phenomenon we don't really know what we're doing yet. An industry that is only 25 years old can hardly be considered mature. We are still figuring stuff out.

I forgot to mention something earlier. In 'normal' income streams, if you forget to kiss your boss's ass you don't get paid. And you always have a boss…

That's why I would go as far as saying that the 4th component of passive income would be keeping ass kissing to a minimum. The less love you need to show the buttocks of the world the more passive the form of income. Just hear me out for a second. Dealing with people can be exhausting. The less human interaction is required by your project the better. Ideally passive income should not be affect by your interactions with employees, bosses or customers.

The thing you made should just sit there and make you money. Unfortunately we do not live in such a world and most forms of income require you to pucker your lips.

It's best we categorize different forms of income.

They can be placed into three categories. Active, Semi-passive and passive.

Active income is income that you have to constantly work for. Earlier we used the example of free lancing. If you don't do, you don't get.

Semi-passive income is income that you have to work for on a consistent basis with much less involvement. You have decent periods of time where you can put your feet up. This is the method that is advocated by most gurus as true passive income. Which of course isn't true.

Passive income is income that you work for once and receive continued compensation for with little or no maintenance. Whether the maintenance is a lot can be defined by the ratio of the incomes lifespan and value compared to the amount of work that needs to be done.

It's a bit repetitive but we need to get this straight.

Up ahead we'll tackle something that most people never consider. The value of active income.

CHAPTER 4: WHY ACTIVE INCOME IS TECHNICALLY BETTER

Now that we have already been introduced to the concept of active income, let's dive a little deeper into it.

This is how people smarter than I explain it:

"Income for which services have been performed. This includes wages, tips, salaries, commissions and income from businesses in which there is material participation."

-Investopedia

What I'm going to do is introduce you to a rule of thumb that not a lot of people know. Mainly because they don't stop to think.

Active income is superior to passive income. Simple. This is because of the dynamics that follow after earning the actual income. Based on the system you use and the decisions you make.

If its passive income your return will always be smaller. And you will work very hard for that small return.

Active income on the other hand falls on you like a mountain. It can be a lot when you finally get your hands on it. When choosing between these two types of income you have to decide whether you want to swap continues small return (passive) for large, once-off, windfalls (active).

This is the part where you might say, "But Max getting a lump sum isn't necessarily better than getting periodic payments. I may even prefer the latter."

No... lump sums are better. More money is better than less money when everything else stays the same.

Let's look at the example of a website. You have decided to build a website and are putting as much effort in it as you can. It takes a while but slowly your website gains traction. You start to become an authority in your field and build a nice little following. More importantly you are now making some income off the site. This income is semi-passive and you don't need to do too much to maintain it.

You're living a small dream come true. The site is giving you a cozy US $1,800 a month. Not enough to make you quit your job, but a serious side income for most people.

Now consider that your website is actually a business. Businesses can be sold. They can change ownership. Websites can be sold on sites like www.flippa.com and www.empireflippers.com. There are a bunch of different criteria that determine the value of your site. The most important one as you already guessed is how much money the website makes.

If you go through these sites you'll notice one thing. The sales price of a website appears to be twenty times that of the monthly income! I find this slightly exorbitant but it looks like people can close the sale with such prices.

You're little website would fetch you $18,000. Saying that you could sell it for $20,000 doesn't seem too far off either. Some "experts" say that the sales price of a website should be 2 years of its monthly income.

Now you have a choice. Do you stick with your project and collect the $1,800 every month or do u flog it? It's not an easy call to make. You may still be capable of increasing site revenue. What do you do?

Practically speaking the only thing that matters is money coming into your pocket. One thing you need to learn and realize is the critical mass of money. That is, the point where money starts making more money. That point is not having

$1,000, $2,000, or $3,000 in your bank account. You can, however, reach that point with a twenty grand. This will sound stupid but the buying power of $1,800 is not the same as that of $20,000. You can do more with more money. That includes investing and starting other ventures.

Staying with internet business. If you sold your website, you now have the capital to go into e-commerce. You literally have enough money to engage factories to produce for you and you can sell your products on Amazon. If done sensibly, in another 18 months that $20,000 should have tripled.

What you have done is exchanged your passive income side hustle for an active income side hustle that makes vastly more money. AND you don't need to spend that much more time on it.

It's all about upgrading your skill. You are like a money making machine and as you get better you up the game that you play.

Maybe this example doesn't do it for you. Here's another one.

How do people make money in real-estate? Really good money is made by fixing run-down places and flipping them for a significant profit. Another way is to build a property from scratch and sell it. Normally developers will aim to sell the majority of their real-estate and hold on to a smaller portion to receive some passive income as a safety net.

They do this over and over again. Making the company successful or individuals rich. You are never going to get rid of passive income. Its main purpose is to serve as your fallback if things go sour or you don't want to work anymore. Another reason to go after it is because it serves as a hedge (security) against inflation.

Inflation is what happens when little money chases lots of goods. This has the effect that things become more expensive.

In other words, money loses its value over time. This is a constant that happens everywhere. US $1 million from the 1980s is worth about $8 million in today's money. That's horrifying!!

Investing in passive income sources can help you weather the inflation storm. It may not be more valuable but at least it hasn't lost value (or loses little value). This is a bit confusing but we'll cover it in more details later on.

If you take inflation into account it is better to spend money today than hold onto it for a couple of years.

Later we will also see that it takes larger sums of money to get 'real' passive income sources going.

I can't just sit here and trash passive income though. In its own way it's a beautiful thing. Having a safety net is more important to most people than being crazy rich. All you really want to do is be able to feed yourself and your family. Have a roof over your head and have enough money for some comfort and entertainment.

It also gives you time to work on other things. You can spend a day with your kids. You can learn to sculpt. You can work on community projects and things you deeply care about.

Your goal should be to have a mixed income model. You need both active, semi-passive and completely passive income in your portfolio. This mix will give you the highest returns and greatest amount of freedom. What exactly this mix looks like no one can decide for you. That's a personal lifestyle decision.

Just remember that passive income can never make you rich on its own.

Let's go over income sources that can be defined as semi-passive.

CHAPTER 5: SEMI PASSIVE INCOME SOURCES

We shouldn't leave the types of passive income up to the imagination. In this section, let's look at sources that could be considered as semi-passive income.

These are mistaken for real passive income. You will have heard of most of them, if you've already done your research on the subject.

WEBSITES (ONLINE BUSINESS)

One thing you have to love about the American spirit is how it finds new ways to innovate in business. Other nations might be excellent at science and engineering but The US has always been excellent at driving small enterprise growth. You can see this by how the internet has been incorporated into business culture.

The US pretty much came up with the idea of making money through the web and location independent businesses. One of the biggest innovations that has been pushed on the internet is decentralization. We don't need to depend on big companies anymore. We can run a very successful venture with little manpower and start-up capital. You don't need to be big to be able to compete in the modern marketplace.

A website is different because most of the interaction you have with customers and audiences are not in real time. Stuff kind of just sits on the website and people come and go when they please. There is also little direct interaction with the customer. You don't need to meet face to face and talk things over.

These characteristics shape the way we make money online. You create a product and automate the marketing and purchasing process. This means you don't even need to be awake when the sales happen.

The cool thing is you can do this with most products and most services. So the potential is huge. But you already knew that.

The question is, "if it's so great why is it only semi-passive income?"

Lots of gurus claim that this is the ultimate passive income source. That's rubbish.

We can ignore the fact that it takes a while to set up and get things going. Remember that extensive work at the beginning is a prerequisite for passive income.

Afterwards it's all a question of maintenance.

You may be thinking about starting a blog. Once you've gained an audience than all you need to do is monetize it and you have a passive income stream. There is one small weakness with this reasoning. People will come to your blog for the free content you're providing. You pumping out free stuff on a regular basis. If you stop working your audience numbers will drop. You will still have people coming in but your income will decrease. In the best case scenario it will stagnate.

So you need to be active for most websites to have success.

Another good example is podcasting. Podcasting has been all the rage over the past few years. Everybody's doing it. In fact you may know a pensioner who just got into it. That's how popular it is. Podcasting is like an internet radio show where you can listen to the show any time you want.

This is normally what happens. You start your podcast talking about all the things you find awesome. Once in a while you have guests over that you interview to keep the content fresh. You're doing a good job and are gaining traction. People are starting to notice you and you build a proper audience.

First of all podcasting is limited because there is no product. You are giving away the podcast for free so you don't get paid. The only way to make money with podcasts is to sell your own stuff or give relevant companies ad time. So you endorse their products and talk about them for some 5 minutes. The problem is that you only get paid once for this. You get paid every time you mention the company or product.

This isn't great because the show will have a back log. There are going to be people who find your podcast out of the blue and decide to binge on every single episode. These guys are going to hear those ads, which means that over the life time of your podcast what you've been paid for ads decreases as your listener base increases.

Confused? That's ok, I didn't get it at first either.

Let's take a simple example. You have 100 listeners in August 2015. Company ABC is paying you $100 for an ad. The company essentially paid $1 for every listener. You rock your show and in August 2016 you have 1000 listeners. That means you have 900 new listeners. All of a sudden that $100 has paid for 1000 persons, making the long term cost look more like 10 cents per listener. This is great for the advertisers but makes you look a little silly.

Podcast income is not passive. You have to work for it day-in-day out. Even worse, the money you make today is peanuts if you think of the future.

This is my rant on why you don't podcast for money.

However to be fair that money could be very useful if invested wisely. This goes back to the principle that active income is worth more at a single point in time. The issue is that it takes a lot (and I mean a lot) of work to bring a podcast to a level where ad income is really big.

The most successful 'podcaster' doing this is a guy called Joe Rogan, whose show is just about random stuff. The difference is that he podcasts multiple times a week. On average his podcasts run about 3 hours long. His hard work has paid off as "The Joe Rogan Experience" is downloaded more than 7 million times every month. Because of this the man gets very good money from companies advertising with him.

Going back to the issue of websites. The major reason why they are only semi-passive is because of the work that goes into actually making one successful. As you can see from the previous examples things get much more complicated when taking the value over time into consideration.

However, websites are a sort of 'Holy Grail' for wannabe entrepreneurs. The internet cuts down on costs like no other channel can. It gives you access to an international market right from the get go.

With a bit of work you can put a system in place that is virtually passive. This only applies to certain cases but is possible. YET...even in those circumstances online business is not completely passive. Yes, the production has been taken care of. Yes, the distribution has been taken care of. One thing that will always require your watchful eye on it is marketing.

You will need to insure that traffic is driven to your site. You need people to see your product or service otherwise you can't sell them anything in the first place. It all comes back to having to do some work. In many cases more work than you might imagine.

If you're interested in the basics of online business check out my booklet, "Online Business The 4 Major Methods: How to make $800 and avoid the lies told by online gurus."

Source: Websites

Start-up Capital: **2/10**

Technical Knowhow: **4/10**

Income Lifespan: **3/10**

Value of Income: **4/10**

Degree of Passiveness: **3/10**

Overall Difficulty: **3/10**

SOFTWARE

Software is closely related to websites and online business. In some ways it even falls under online business entirely. This is because it can easily be distributed over the internet. Ones and zeros, the bits and bytes that make up programs. Let's look at it from a more traditional perspective to make some distinction.

The world has become computerized to a point where farmers in the outback of Kenya are using mobile phones to makes and receive payments. It doesn't matter what country you go to you will find somebody who is using WhatsApp. I'm no too sure about North Korea but you get what I'm trying to say!

It's not only about mobile phones. All sorts of computing devices are becoming more common throughout the world. Each and every one of them needs software to function.

Not having the technical skills matters less and less. There are specialists for hire from around the globe who are willing to work with you for the right price. With a bit of sweat you can put together your own software. It could be an app, a game or a web services.

Using the power of the internet you can sell your products to your target customers. This can be somewhat passive. Apart from marketing, you're pretty much putting up your legs waiting for money to role in. As mentioned before, marketing is not a picnic.

We live in a world of faster and better. Everything around us is always improving itself. Customer behavior has changed over the past few decades. When something new is on the market they don't want it today, they wanted it yesterday. You can never move quick enough to keep up with demand, even if people didn't know they want something.

This sort of attitude mixed with a world where the internet is available to many people has led to one problem for software. It needs to be updated constantly. Commercial suicide is what you call not releasing regular updates for your app.

It goes as far as to affect the quality of product that companies put out on the market. They release programs full of bugs thinking that everything can be fixed by updating them later. Before the internet every company (small and large) would put their stuff through its paces. If the product was faulty it would come back to bite them very quickly. In some ways this is actually an advantage for developers.

Basically, dealing with software is a hustle just like any other business. That's what we have to realize about all these methods that are taught as passive income. What you're trying to do is either build a portfolio or a business. Either requires you to gain the skill to make it happen.

You could release a software that makes you some money without updating it. The thing is that if you don't update it. If you don't do your maintenance. That income source is going to be short lived and won't meet the requirement we have set for passive income.

Software is a volume game with a lot of potential if you do it right.

Source: Software

Start-up Capital: **3/10**

Technical Knowhow: **4/10**

Income Lifespan: **3/10**

Value of Income: **5/10**

Degree of Passiveness: **3/10**

Overall Difficulty: **4/10**

HIRING OUT GOODS (EQUIPMENT RENTAL)

We're going to bring it back to the physical world for a moment. If you want semi passive income you can do something that people have been doing for a long time. You can hire out something in return for payment.

Not everyone wants to spend their hard earned money buying expensive things they are just going to use once or twice a year. You can use this to your advantage. Buy what others want and rent it out to them. It's a small commitment for them which satisfies their needs. For you it's a nice little side business.

The crux of it all is what product you are going to offer.

You want to go after something that has demand. People need to want what you're offering. The product should have a good functional lifespan. A warranty for a couple of years comes to mind. This means that you might need to dig deeper into your pocket. Better warranties (and thus longer working lives) tend to come with higher quality and more expense.

This is a business heavily dependent of geography. No, not the high school subject. But your surrounding area. People need to come to you and pick the stuff up themselves. You can get some customers over the internet but they need to be local.

Scaffolding for smaller construction jobs is a good example. If you live in an area where there is a good amount of construction going on you could capitalize on this. Just because there're big boys involved in a business that doesn't automatically mean that you can't compete. Lots of local people and businesses would be happy to give you a shot. There's something special about buying from a smaller business as compared to buying from large corporates.

Scaffolding is great because the product may very well outlast you. You won't need to worry much about the maintenance. They are metal poles that stick together. So long you don't have a 25 year old rust creeping up you should be fine. The product can even be abused for fun without affecting sales price. Try throwing some poles of your roof into your neighbor's yard to see if you can kill their annoying cat. It shouldn't take much damage really. You can always lie that it was an accident.

Another example is technology. It's surprising that in today's world you can still make money renting out laptops, projectors and printers. Not every business needs these items permanently. There are other items out there like cars, furniture, building equipment, the list goes on and on.

This is interesting because it kind of fits into something that a lot of people are excited about. The sharing economy. Sharing what you have with another for monetary compensation. Uber is a well-known start-up. With Uber you can act as a taxi driver whenever you feel like it, using your own car. People can request a pick up and you can decide whether you're interested or not. Normally the rates are competitive and the actual taxi drivers hate this company's guts.

More importantly hiring stuff out is a more passive activity.

It is in no way as passive as building a website, but the income is semi-passive. What you need to do is find a rhythm that lets you spend less time on this sort of business. The easiest way to do this would be to find items that you can hire out for an extended period of time.

<u>Source: Hiring Out Goods</u>

Start-up Capital: **4/10**

Technical Knowhow: **3/10**

Income Lifespan: **3/10**

Value of Income: **5/10**

Degree of Passiveness: **2/10**

Overall Difficulty: **4/10**

REAL-ESTATE

You knew this was bound to be included on the list somewhere. Real-estate is the original passive income method. Really exciting stuff. There's something wonderful about seeing a project take physical shape. With real-estate you get to touch your hard work. It will last for decades and provide you and others with all sorts of memories.

An interesting historical fact is the origins of the word "landlord". A person who is in charge of a property. He or she is the one that collects all that sweet rent money. The word literally refers to being the lord of a piece of land.

In Europe a long time ago, back in the ages of kings and queens you had persons who were given custody of land. All the land belonged to the king but he would dish it out to the ruling elite. The princes, barons, lords and dukes. These nobles would then in turn give the land to farmers and the general population.

Every now and again these tenants would have to pay a tribute to the landlord for the right to use the property. This could have been done with money, produce or labor. That's why nobles where so powerful, because they indirectly had control of all the resources of the land.

What does this teach us? That land is valuable. It always has been and always will be.

Real-estate is a bit tricky. Not only in the sense of legal issues but the sheer capital one needs. That makes it a less accessible form of income for most people.

The basics are easy to understand. Buy or build a house. Put it on rent. Collect passive income. The problem with being a landlord is that it is not as passive as you might think. Dealing with tenants is a headache. Managing your relationship with real-estate agents is bothersome. Meeting all the legal requirements is a nightmare. It can be quite the experience.

If you have a property on rent pray to God that the tenants are rich, decent and clean people. That's where most of the maintenance comes in. An unruly tenant can make what is supposed to be a breeze into a hail storm. With a decent person renting from you there will likely be an issue every 3 months or so that needs to be sorted out. This turns into a weekly affair if you're unlucky.

In the worst case scenario they will damage your property. It's surprisingly easy to do thousands of dollars' worth of damage within an extended period of time. Real-estate is still an excellent source of passive income though.

Let's quickly tackle what may be the biggest challenge concerning this, capital. You need money to get into this game. That can't be avoided. You will pay sooner or later. The best advice I was given by an elderly gent on this was, "don't take up a loan you can't pay back". It's rare that someone is capable of putting the money together to buy a property in cash. Credit is a beautiful thing. It's just that when it goes wrong it can really go wrong.

The way that a lot of people recommend to go is to get a mortgage to buy a house and then pay back the money with rent that comes in. Let's say your mortgage is $550 a month and you can put the place on rent for $1,000. That means in one swipe you can pay your mortgage and collect $450 dollars. That doesn't sound half bad.

There is more to it however. Most of us will have experienced what can happen if a market crashes. What happened when the real-estate bubble in 2008 melted down the global economy? Can you imagine that because of a bunch of bad loans to American banks, the mines in my home country of Zambia fired thousands of workers? Crazy chain reaction.

We want to be able to shield ourselves as much as possible from such disasters. One way to do this is to buy a fixer-upper. A property that's rundown that you fix up so it's livable again. Like this you can get a bargain deal.

A house that should have cost $250,000 may cost $125,000. Once you're done with the renovations you may have spent $45,000. Now you have a house that's worth $250,000 which you only spent $170,000 on. The dynamics may lead you to need more cash in hand for this method but the profit potential is greater.

This also leads to you being able to take a hit. If the market falls and your house is now worth $195,000 you are still in the green.

The above example is obviously very simplified. Check out some real-estate experts for more on this.

What's done a lot in developing countries is even simpler. The process looks like this:

-Save money.
-Buy land.
-Build house.
-Get building loan to do interior.
-Finish house.
-Put house on rent.
-Pay loan off using rent.
-Go party.

Instead of buying a house you actually build one. The end result is a significant cost saving. You only go out to get a loan to do the last part of the house. This way you guarantee that the loan is being put to good use and you're quickly put into a position to pay it back using rentals.

It's a bit intimidating. You'd have to do your own due diligence to check whether this can work for you. It took my parents nine years to build their house this way. All without loans. It's hilarious how long it took, and to be honest they weren't serious enough with the project. From my estimation it could have been done in three years. It's all about long term perspective and weighing the pros and cons.

Don't let your thinking be narrowed when you consider real-estate as your passive income sources. There are other options than just building a house or buying an apartment.

You could go into commercial real-estate. Businesses need a place to perch too. This way you can target a very specific market. It doesn't have to be shop lots either. Some smart people are starting to rent out their properties on a time share basis.

You can build a professional kitchen with all the necessary equipment and facilities that chefs could want. From there on you can rent time slots to small entrepreneurs who need access to such facilities. This maybe 2 days a week or so. Your job is to market your business until all the time slots are filled up. This is more of the sharing economy, just in an old fashioned way.

If money is an issue with you as it is with most people you can also try to think small. In college we lived in a condominium complex. Only one of my housemates had a car. He quickly sold it saying that he really didn't need it. Now I was stuck with an empty parking slot. I didn't think much of it until I heard that one of my friends had been renting his parking slot out for about $35 a month. That's not $35 in the US or Australia by the way. That was $35 in South East Asia. Best of all it was extremely passive income.

Lastly I do need to mention the extraction industry, which is also called the primary sector. It may seem a bit off but it has everything to do with real-estate and semi-passive income.

You or your family may have a large piece of land somewhere in the middle of nowhere. Land is always valuable no matter how far outside of the city it might be. You just need to find what exactly is valuable about that particular piece of land. A property surveyed for minerals can turn up all sorts of interesting things. Precious stones, semi-precious stones, and in rare cases oil. The property may not even cost so much because of where it is.

You don't have to be involved in the actual running of a mine. All you need are the title deeds and the necessary rights. You can approach companies telling them, "You do all the work and give me a small cut." If the figures look right they'll jump on it.

This is what has happened in across the United States recently. With the advancements in technology, "fracking" has brought a new way to access gas and oil that was stuck in bedrock layers. People literally make deals with company's one month and buy themselves Cadillac's the next month. It's quite disgusting really. I'm a bit of an environmentalist so I want to hate fracking... and I do. BUT no one can deny how appetizing of a business opportunity it is for land owners.

There's more to it then what's underground though. We mustn't forget the forests that come with large pieces of land. Certain trees have commercial value. Timber companies would be willing to sign a deal with you if the greenery meets their standards.

Depending on the type of tree it can take 7-40 years to mature. That means your family would cash in anywhere from once to 10 times in a generation. This may not sound like much but we are talking about hundreds of thousands of dollars that you essentially did no work for. You are simply the custodian of the land. The landlord.

Source: Real-Estate

Start-up Capital: *7/10*

Technical Knowhow: *5/10*

Income Lifespan: *9/10*

Value of Income: *3/10*

Degree of Passiveness: *7/10*

Overall Difficulty: *6/10*

BUSINESS

We can't forget about actual business when talking about passive income. Most of the methods that we've mentioned up until now are businesses geared towards automation. Who's to say you can't do this for every type of business out there? This is what Tim Ferriss was pushing.

As a business owner, one of your goals should be to be to work only as long as you want. For some people that means 60 hour work weeks. For most of us that means doing 3 hours of work every day, followed by random escapades.

This requires great skill and discipline. You have to detach yourself from your business. The coffee shop isn't your baby anymore. At the beginning it might have been, but like children businesses grow up and take up a life of their own.

Once you do this you will find it much easier to delegate work. You start to trust your employees more than you used too. This isn't blind "steal all my money" trust, it's trusting that they'll get the job done.

Eventually you will want someone to manage your business for you. A business owner doesn't have to be a manager after all. Talent can be sourced from within our outside of your organization. All that matters it that the person fits the role he is being assigned.

Step by step you build a system that automates the workings of your business. There is still work to be done on your end. This makes the whole set up semi-passive. The system itself is based on technology and people. Technology will make things easier all round but some tasks can only be completed by a real life person.

The point is that the best entrepreneurs on this planet don't need to be in the office to run a successful company. Look at Sir Richard Branson. The man is running an international conglomerate. There seems to be a Virgin branded company for everything. There is no way that he is involved in the day to day running of each and every company.

Virgin Atlantic, Virgin Galactic, Virgin Mobile, Virgin Megastores, Virgin Care, bla bla bla. The Virgin Group has more than 30 subsidiaries. They employ approximately 50,000 people.

Branson only has one option in such a situation and that is to automate the running of his businesses. It becomes a passive venture by nature because he is only one man. We on the other hand want to build businesses that become passive ventures by force.

Small guys like us don't need to look at building complicated company hierarchies. We can outsource what can be outsourced to make things easier on us. This is a skill in itself but it's entirely possible. You don't take you rubbish to the rubbish dump yourself do you? You pay someone else to. It may be a company or it may be the local council. Either way you pay in subscription or tax.

Outsourcing can make a lot of sense. Sometimes...

The following chapter is going to tackle income sources that are highly passive. This is the dream we've all been lusting after.

Source: Business

Start-up Capital: *5/10*

Technical Knowhow: *9/10*

Income Lifespan: *7/10*

Value of Income: *10/10*

Degree of Passiveness: *2/10*

Overall Difficulty: *8/1*

CHAPTER 6: PASSIVE INCOME SOURCES

Now we get to the topic we all love so much. There's a catch though (isn't there always). You won't love this as much as you might think. Passive income is not what it's cracked up to be. It's great. It just happens that it is a lot less accessible then you'd imagine.

That could be one way to define the difference between active, semi-passive and passive income. The more passive a source of income the less accessible it is to the general public.

You need to be hard working and innovative to get this far. Passive income is like the reward for becoming a high earning individual. "You have quite a bit of money. Why don't you invest it in real passive income so you're secure for the rest of your life"?

It's a bit depressing if you think about it like that. Most people won't reach the level where they can go after real passive income sources. It's something everybody should have access to but it's reserved for a select few.

Maybe by arming yourself with some knowledge we can change that. At least I'd like to think so...

STOCKS
We've all heard of the marvels of the stock market. How this one random dude from a town in the middle of nowhere came to New York and made a fortune. Reality looks a little bit different.

First of all the stock market is a place where you can buy a tiny share of a company. This way you end up becoming a part owner, what they call a shareholder. Normal people do this through other companies such as hedge funds because the amounts that need to be invested are big.

The stock market is a monster! There is no better way to put it. If you don't know what you're doing you're going to be eaten alive, regurgitated, eaten again, digested and expelled.

Unless your job is feeding this monster. Don't play around with it. Someone who's involved with Wallstreet or whose life revolves around the DAX can do what he wants. They know better than most of us (hint: insider information) and if they don't their career will be very short.

We are interested only in what stocks can do for us with passive income in mind. That being said the stock market is an excellent way to make passive income. It is one of the few 100% passive income sources out there.

I have shares in a small company called CEC, Copperbelt Energy Corporation. They are involved in transmitting electricity to the mining sector in my country. The shares are a very small number that I obtained from their Initial public offering (IPO). This is when companies first list on the stock market and make their shares available to the public.

After about a year I had utterly forgotten about the whole deal. Then I got a cheque in the mail worth about $90. For a second I thought someone had made a mistake. Then it clicked. I shrugged it off cause it was such a small sum but it did make me smile for a couple of days.

The initial investment was about $1,100. To be honest I don't remember the exact figure, it was nearly a decade ago. That meant a return of about 8.2%. That's pretty good.

The thing is that you need a lot of money to benefit of stocks. Let's say you want $3,000 every month for your upkeep. That means you need $36,000 for the entire year. To get such dividends at an 8% return you would need to invest a total $450,000.You'll probably need to increase this number a bit to

THE PASSIVE INCOME LIE

cover charges and inflation. Let's say about $600,000 (which is a bit more than a bit).

This is entirely possible if you put your mind to it. Many people's houses cost more than $600,000. If you can put a house together you can hustle to find a way to make your stocks happen.

The great thing is that there is no maintenance for you what so ever. ZERO.

Now you're collecting $3,000 every month and you haven't contributed anything in the terms of work.

The trick with the stock market is to be boring. The more boring your investment strategy the more it is likely to succeed and make you passive income.

This is best outlined in a book written by Benjamin Graham, "The Intelligent Investor". The only book you'll ever need where the stock market is concerned. It comes highly recommended by value investors like Warren Buffet.

Practicing self-discipline is the most important thing. Don't play around with your investment and start speculating. Think long term. You're investing with the next 20 years in mind.

Now you may ask yourself questions about risk and safety with the stock market collapsing a couple of years back. You're right to be worried. There is a simple way to get over this hurdle. It's called dollar cost averaging.

Dollar cost averaging is when you invest in stocks on a regular basis over an extended period of time, always at the same cost. You are not just investing in any stock, you're investing in the entire stock market. You can do this by using instruments called index funds, the most famous of which is the S&P 500.

If you put $1,000 every month into an index fund they will take the $1,000 and more or less spread it throughout the entire market they are targeting. Since the market is dynamic the number of shares you can get for your $1,000 will sometimes be more and sometimes be less. This coupled with the fact that you're constantly increasing your shareholdings ends up protecting you against market down turns.

Analysis of the market crash of 2008/2009 have shown that persons who used this method through the rough times actually grew their investments worth by 4%. That's 4% growth when everything around you is going to heck! People are killing themselves because they've lost everything and you actually made money!!

Earlier I said it's an easy method. Maybe that's an exaggeration. Being disciplined is never easy. You just need to know that you have the option. The stock market is not just for the ultra-rich. The catch is that you first need the money to invest. Ideally you need a good source of active income so you can take advantage of dollar cost averaging.

Not all experts agree with this strategy but most do. I recommend you read Graham's book if you're interested in this topic.

Do you due diligence not only about general stock investing but about hedge funds, index funds and private equity. There's a lot of stuff out there so make sure to understand the basics from the start.

Source: Stocks

Start-up Capital: **3-10/10**

Technical Knowhow: **4-10/10**

Income Lifespan: **9/10**

Value of Income: **2/10**

Degree of Passiveness: **10/10**

Overall Difficulty: **6/10**

TECHNICAL POSITIONS

I struggled to find a name for this passive income method. It's one of those awkward things you wouldn't know about unless you've been told.

There're some instances when you kind out just sit there, do little to no work at all and someone will give you money. It's not magic. It's taking advantage of policies governing the way we run business. Usually you have to have a reputation and be an expert in a field to do this.

Every company has shareholders. You know that. Every company also has a board of directors. You also know that. What you might not know is that the board of directors receive a sitting allowance when they fulfill their obligation to the company. That obligation involves sitting, having tea and talking about business. So these people get paid for doing what every working person on this planet does (sometimes).

The board meets once or twice a year depending on the company's constitution. Sometimes more if there is some sort of crisis. The best thing is that the board rarely gets blamed if the company gets in trouble. That's the CEO's job, who by the way, is chosen by the board.

It's a cushy little job. Imagine meeting once a year. You go and discuss some issues for about 2 hours and then the company pays you $5,000. It will likely be more depending on the size of the organization. To me it even feels like a scam of sorts. The board are supposed to have the business's best interest at heart. That's why they are given so much power when they act together. Yet all they do is talk, and maybe give some advice.

Anyway that's the way that limited and public companies are set up.

Like already mentioned you normally have to have some sort of standing to be asked to join the board. This goes back to what was said earlier. Passive income is for those who are already somewhat successful. This might be you a few years from now.

A better example and more attainable for the lay man is ownership in a business. Not just any ownership but the kind where you do nothing and get paid.

In Dubai they have a little law that makes the locals big money. Any business that wants to open shop in the emirate must be 51% locally owned. This means that every single business must have an Emirati partner. Most of the time these guys don't do anything. Their job is to sign some papers and collect a pay cheque at the end of the month. All the work is done by whoever started the business in the first place.

This is one of the reasons the locals are so rich in Dubai.

Another country that has similar policies is Malaysia. You need a Malaysian partner if you want to do business in the country. Generally the exact same thing happens here as it does in Dubai. It's a great way to make your people rich with little work. If you have a market others want to play in...

Now if your country doesn't have such policies in place don't fret. You can achieve something similar by actually working for it. This way you get to feel good about the money you're earning.

There's something called a sleeping partner. No, it doesn't refer to a lazy spouse! This is a person who has invested into a business and is not involved in the day to day running. When the time comes he or she gets their cut of the profit, which is less than the persons involved in operating the business.

The interesting thing is that you don't need money to do this. Money is the preferred medium of value but you can also give something that might be just as good. If you have property that is not being used you can give it to your partners so they can run the business from there. Maybe you have an amazing network and you can hook up some long term contracts from valuable clients. It could also be that you helped the business overcome technical issues such as registration and licensing.

Having a technical position is an interesting way to make passive income.

Source: Technical Positions

Start-up Capital: *1/10*

Technical Knowhow: *8/10*

Income Lifespan: *6/10*

Value of Income: *3/10*

Degree of Passiveness: *8/10*

Overall Difficulty: *7/10*

PENSION FUNDS

People forget about this. Everybody should have a pension. Maybe it's because you need to wait a couple of decades to enjoy the fruits of your labor. It's understandable how that may turn you off. In most countries it's law to contribute to some sort of pension scheme though.

In the US you're looking at the 401K in the UK it's called the State Pension. Wherever you are one of your goals in life should be to max out you pension fund. This way when you're finally ready to "officially" retire you'll have something in the piggy bank. This is not a major goal as inflation tends to eat away part of your pension.

I also say officially because someone who loves their job may not want to retire. What you're really doing is saying you retire so that you can collect your pension and then go on work 5 to 8 hours a day anyway. Being old should be fun. There's no reason to make your life seem like less than it is worth.

Unfortunately politics can affect your state pension.

As I'm writing this chapter there is a big problem in Europe. Well the truth is there is a significant problem in Greece. To make a very long story short Greece is broke! Broke to the point that they closed all banks for one week because there was basically no money in the country.

To fix this problem Greece is borrowing a lot of money from the rest of the EU. Billions and billions of Euro. This money mainly comes from countries like Holland and the big fish Germany. Now you have to ask yourself where these nations are get that money from. Is it just lying around? Don't they need it? The cold hard answer is ...they are taking it away from their citizens. The money that ordinary people are giving to their government for taxes and pensions is being used to bail out Greece!

This includes the pensions of young, middle-aged and old Germans and Dutch. This could lead to a dark future, especially for today's working youth. A person who is 30 today may run into problems getting their pension when he or she is 67.

The same principle applies to the US bailing out the banks a couple of years back.

These dynamics make pensions a bit tricky. The best thing you can do is not depend completely on what you are owed by the pension authority. You are likely to get something but for safety reasons you want to grow other forms of semi-passive and passive income to support you in your old age.

So a pension, whether it comes from the state or a private company, is only supplemental income.

Source: Pension Funds

Start-up Capital: *5/10*

Technical Knowhow: *2/10*

Income Lifespan: *10/10*

Value of Income: *5/10*

Degree of Passiveness: *10/10*

Overall Difficulty: *7/10*

INTELLECTUAL PROPERTY

This is a topic that really excites me. And it might excite you too! Why? Intellectual property (IP) is the best sort of passive income!! That's my biased opinion of course.

The foundation of this all lies in having an idea. The idea that you created should be valuable to a paying market, and if it's packaged & marketed the right way that will turn into monetary value. One of the great things about IP is that it can make you money for a long time! On average you hold the rights to your IP for a minimum of 25 years. That's 25 years of potential cash inflow!

Take this booklet for example. I hold what is called the 'copyright' to it. That means it cannot be commercially reproduced without my consent. If it is, I will be compensated according to the agreement with whoever buys the publishing rights. Copyrights for literature typically last 75 years. This book is mine for as long as I live (unless I live to be 101).

As mentioned before. Your idea needs to have proper commercial value. This value is determined by the market and not by you. There needs to be demand which is defined by the willingness and ability to buy the product.

Ideally your idea should also have staying power. It should be as evergreen as possible. Good fiction literature never goes out of fashion. Ask Goethe or Shakespeare. Their works are still read by millions! Mozart or Vivaldi on the other hand are having a tough time in today's world. Think about it, one day all this electronic stuff you're hearing will be called classical music!

IP works on royalties. This means you get a small percentage of sales whenever your product is bought.

Since IP is all about ideas, you can own systems as well. An example of this is a franchise. McDonalds HQ doesn't run every single stores around the world. They give budding entrepreneurs the right to use their name and system. The McDonalds fast food chain is a proven system on how to make money in fast food. Do things exactly like they tell you and your business will be a success. At least that's how it's meant to work.

If you're trying to set up your own McDonalds you need to pay $45,000 to get the rights not to mention the actual cost of setting up the restaurant. This are about $2.5 million. Then you have to pay 12% of you profit to McDonalds at the end of every year. This is why franchises are so successful. It's not so much about the service or product but about the intellectual property!

Let's not forget about having those great invention ideas. I believe that everybody has about four great ideas every year that could make you really good money if you put them into action. That means you have likely had a number of good product ideas to.

Most product developers and inventors go the route of trying to build their own prototype and later on their own business. You can do this if you're up for it. Heck if you trust yourself and market yourself right you could end up on the Shark Tank! The problem with this approach is that it is time, capital and labor intensive.

Another way to do it is to sell licensing to businesses without making the stuff yourself. Lots of people don't like this because they feel that their idea will get miss handled and that they can make more money if they do it themselves. If you're one of these persons I'd have to ask you to get off you high horse before you hurt yourself! No really, let's think about this from a different angle...

Why bother setting up production facilities, create distribution channels and convincing customers to try and buy your product when someone else can to it for you? Yes, you would make less money. That's not the objective though! The objective is to make passive income.

The best resource I have come across for learning the process of bringing your idea to market is a book by Stephen Key called "One Simple Idea". Key was involved in the creation of laser tag and dozens of other products. Some made him millions, some made him tens of thousands. All of it was passive income!

The really valuable thing about IP is the fact that anyone can get involved in it. There's nothing stopping your 12 year old from writing a song is there? Financially the major barrier is paying for the rights. Patents can costs thousands of dollars. Interestingly enough you can get a temporary patent for a one year period for $65 in the US, so there are way to deal with these issue.

If there is one challenge with IP it is that people don't believe in themselves. Were ideas are concerned, many think it is only for 'creative' people. For some reason most of us feel that we don't fall under that category.

The best advice I've been given is to try it out. Write your book, sing your song, and sketch your idea. See where it takes you. Once you start on the path you'll look at things differently! You will find new ways to tackle the challenge. Eventually you will find a way to break it down into smaller parts. Now you're not dealing with a big problem but with many small ones. Solve them one at a time, one after another. Step by step.

Consider what you can do with intellectual property! It's a proper form of passive income. It is also accessible to ordinary people.

Source: Intellectual Property

Start-up Capital: **3/10**

Technical Knowhow: **5/10**

Income Lifespan: **9/10**

Value of Income: **2-8/10**

Degree of Passiveness: **10/10**

Overall Difficulty: **5/1**

CHAPTER 7: THE VALUE OF A SYSTEM

There's a concept that keeps on showing up throughout this booklet. That is if you do things right you can set up a system that makes things easier for yourself. The system is what will end up making an income source more passive.

With the right planning, execution and a bit of luck you can turn what is semi-passive income into passive income. This doesn't always work but imagine what your life would be like if it does.

There's a catch. It not easy. I sound like a broken record. On top of that, the system that you do create has to be monitored. Whenever something happens that you didn't count on that the system can't handle, you have to make adjustments. Bit by bit you can get to a nearly passive scenario.

It's all about trial and error.

Treat every passive income stream you're pursuing as a serious business venture. A simple mindset change like this can help you come up with your own solutions to your problems.

A website can be easy to turn into passive income if it meets certain prerequisites. It's a challenge to bring it up to that level! There is a guy called Pat Flynn who is quite famous in the online business community. His main site www.smartpassiveincome.com is an excellent resource on getting started with online business.

When you look at his homepage you'll see that he makes over $100,000 a month. That doesn't really matter. What matters is that in his income report there are two items that stand out. They are both websites. The first is www.securityguardtraininghq.com and the other is www.greenexamacademy.com. They 'only' bring in over $2,000 each. That's a good $4,000 of re-occurring income.

These websites stand out even though they make-up only a tiny fraction of his total income because they are truly passive. The content has not been properly updated in years. I think Pat even forgets they exist sometimes.

He achieved this because each website cemented its authority in its particular niche and the content on it is evergreen. It was relevant yesterday, it is relevant today and will be relevant tomorrow.

When they were first started it was easier to achieve such a position. Now things are different. It should still be possible to achieve this though. To be honest, I can't think of any example to give you of websites started around 2013/2014 that have managed this. It's becoming more and more of a niche game and being active on channels like social media matters.

If you have a more recent example you can email me at max@ingenuitypool.com. I'd love to add any interesting cases to this section.

Real-estate can also become very passive income. It's much easier to achieve. All you need to do is hire a reputable company to deal with the maintenance and collection issues. They will take a cut of the rent and you don't have to worry about anything. Reputation is rather important here. You want to go to a company that is recommended by sensible people. Check the net but always verify with offline sources.

Do not do this over a lawyer. Lawyers are sharks and when they smell blood they take advantage! If you are a lawyer or are going to be one, take this as a compliment. Certain lawyers (the ones that are genetically closer to weasels than humans) will find a way to make you rack up a crazy high legal bill. When you can't pay these exorbitant bills they go to the court demanding your property as compensation. This happens everywhere and its one method that crooked legal practitioners use to build their own little real-estate empire!

When hiring out goods is considered you could go into the leasing game. Now we're talking about bigger machinery here. Stuff that will last for years to come! The barrier as always is that you need a lot more capital to do this. On the other hand because your customers are businesses and because of the dynamics involved in leasing, it may be a safer option than its little cousin (i.e. equipment rental).

Business can be a source of passive income in general once you have reached a point of maturity. The key is patience and having the skill to not interfere with the day to day running. Even if you could do it better.

Achieving all this will take some crazy ingenuity but others have done it before. Why not you? Nobody is better than you, they just know something you don't. There's no reason you can't mimic their system and success. Just go out there and make it happen!

From the sources we've gone over, at least one of them should be within your grasp. At the end of the day it's all about you

CHAPTER 8: WHAT DO YOU REALLY WANT?

This is what it boils done to! What sort of life do you want to live? What sort of income do you need for that lifestyle?

What do you really want?

Do you want an alternative source of income to supplement what you get from your current job or do you want passive income? As we discovered, these are two entirely different things!

In closing we're going to look at a concept from Robert Kiyosaki. Remember the fellow from 'Rich Dad, Poor Dad'? I hate on him a lot but there is one thing he mentioned that was very solid. The idea of the cash flow quadrant.

He states that as a person you fall into one of these quadrants at any time of your financial life. An employee, a self-employed person, a business owner or an investor. That is literally the progression of how you develop your income. You begin of as an employee, start your own freelance thing, that thing evolves into a business, eventually it makes you enough money to start investing.

What you can take home from this progression is that as you move up the ladder from employee to investor it becomes easier for you to take advantage of passive income sources.

The easiest way to build passive income is to first have a lot of money!

You can get this money by starting a business that brings in a good deal of active income. As mentioned at the beginning of this booklet, passive income is more of a hedging system to secure your standard of living.

Going back to the title question, you have to know where you want to be! There is nothing wrong with working for someone.

The majority of the world does and if you do it right you don't have to feel depressed or oppressed.

Many people don't want to build a business. What they want is to create a job for themselves. To be self-employed. The stress that comes with being responsible for others can be overwhelming. If you want to build the next Google or Walmart than go for it. If you want to work in the next Google or Walmart, that's fine too!

The real reason anyone wants passive income is comfort. How much is enough for you? We don't really need millions in the bank to be happy do we? What matters most to you?

By understanding what you really want you will know how much passive income you're actually looking for. This will make it easier for you to plan for the road ahead.

Eventually, you will achieve this elusive dream. Be patient, be disciplined and be pragmatic.

Good luck! And happy hunting!

RESOURCES

If you've found this booklet helpful I would love it if you leave an honest review on Amazon for it. Good or bad ...it doesn't matter, as long as it's honest!

It will not only help me but many others like you that are genuinely interested in the truth about passive income.

Visit me at www.ingenuitypool.com for some interesting articles and resources about entrepreneurship and life.

With Gratitude from Your Friend,

Max

BOOKS MENTIONED
Rich Dad, Poor Dad – Robert Kiyosaki (Don't bother)

The 4-Hour Work Week – Tim Ferris

The Intelligent Investor – Benjamin Graham (I recommend the audio version, easier to follow)

One Simple Idea – Stephen Key (must read)

Online Business the 4 Major Methods – Max Musumali (Me!)
http://www.amazon.com/gp/product/B01593T7M4?*Version*=1&*entries*=0

RESOURCES YOU MIGHT LIKE
Online business, The Smart Passive Income Podcast - www.smartpassiveincome.com

Finance and passive income, Financial Samurai – www.financialsamurai.com